JUST ONE TOSS OF A COIN...

DETERMINED
MY DESTINY AND CAN...

UNLOCK THE SECRET
OF YOUR DESTINY

Richard Danks

Ordering Information:

Prime Seven Media
518 Landmann St.
Tomah City, WI 54660

Printed in the United States of America

CONTENTS

PROLOGUE

This memoir will never be complete. Events which I had long forgotten stir up in my mind, and I think, "How did I miss that? Furthermore, events of significance occur daily which could well qualify for inclusion in this memoir. But I must draw the line somewhere.

I want to thank my family, friends, and everyone who helped me with this manuscript. I appreciate the chance to share my life's journey in this book.

I've tried to show that despite setbacks, disappointments, and betrayals, I've found inner strength and resilience to overcome tough times. This memoir spans over eight decades, full of both triumphs and trials.

Throughout the story, there's a message of perseverance. I've been lucky to travel across continents and cultures, experiencing the highs and lows of life. From moments of joy to times of deep despair, my journey reflects a narrative shaped by experience.

This isn't just a story of ups and downs; it's a testament to the human spirit's ability to rise above challenges and embrace endless possibilities. It's a tale of determination, filled with perseverance and courage.

As I write these words, I do so with humility and gratitude, thankful for the inner strength given by my faith. I hope these pages inspire others facing life's challenges. Every part of our journey, no matter how small, adds to the rich tapestry of life, showcasing unwavering determination, and the enduring triumph of the human spirit.

CHAPTER 1

---·◦◦✧◦◦·---

One Toss of a Coin Determined My Destiny

Unbelievable, isn't it? That at the age of 19 I was terrified of being single for all my life. And I was aware that only desperate measures would remedy the situation. But what could I do? I never met girls and if I did, I wouldn't know what to say or do. I agonised over my wretched plight. I decided I needed to do something way beyond anything I could ever think or imagine possible. This thought sowed a seed that would empower me to rise way above all my doubts and apprehensions and do something I never dreamed was possible. Little did I know the repercussions that would ensue as a result.

It all started innocently enough...

Desperate to change my fate, I ventured to the local dance hall, the Hammersmith Palais, which comfortably held around 1000 people. I went twice and enjoyed the music and atmosphere. People everywhere were laughing, dancing, and enjoying themselves. I was happy just to watch everyone and listen to the band play.

On the third night, as I was preparing to go, I looked in my wallet, and to my dismay I discovered that I only had enough money for the bus fare and a couple of drinks, but not enough for the entrance fee.

I was really looking forward to going to the dance and was annoyed at myself for not providing enough for it. I reluctantly proceeded to my bedroom and took out my frustration on a set of weights with which I vigorously exercised. I soon began to sweat and reached for a handkerchief to wipe it away.

To my great surprise, I discovered that under the handkerchief was a coin. The exact amount of the entrance fee to the dance. But it was now getting late. Almost too late to go to the dance hall. Should I go or should I stay in my bedroom? Quick! I had to make up my mind now. So, I decided to toss that coin and if it came up heads, I would go to the dance. If it came up tails, I would stay at home.

Heads it was, so I left for the dance.

I sat down in the crowded hall and looked around. Everyone had partners. Only one girl was sitting on her own. But I was too fearful to approach her. Then a man, who was tall like me, went up to the girl to ask her for a dance. She shook her head and said "No!". That did it for me. There was no way I was going to suffer a similar rejection.

I sat there for a short while, and quite contrary to my natural inclination, I felt a powerful urge to get up and ask the girl to dance. My mind resisted but my body surged towards the girl. I took her hand and steered her to the dance floor. I said, "Let's dance!" Surprisingly, she didn't resist. Her complexion was of a typical English rose with blue eyes, and she spoke with a broad Lancashire accent. When I asked her for her name she replied, "just call me Pat."

After a couple of dances, we went to the bar and chatted over a drink. I was pleased when she agreed to see me again I and went home in good spirits. I was devastated when she didn't show up for our date.

If this wasn't my first and only girl friend, I would just shrug my shoulders and get on with life. I know it sounds weird, but at that time, I sensed our meeting was destined due to several events. Firstly, the tossed coin coming up heads. Secondly, I sat less than two metres from Pat in a hall of 1000 people. Thirdly I chose to use the handkerchief in the cupboard and not my normal inclination to use the one in my pocket.

Oh, the innocence of youth! In hindsight, I smile at the impetuousness of my decision. And who can argue against my decision when I had a fulfilling marriage of 54 years.

I remember Pat saying that she worked as a waitress in an English Language School. So, I found a telephone booth and systematically flipped through the Yellow Pages for language schools. I was horrified to learn that there were hundreds of them.

I laboriously rang them one by one. It must have been over an hour before I finally found one company that had a Pat Heap working for them. But the man who answered the phone was unwilling to help and simply said, "Sorry, she's very busy with dinners and can't talk to you."

I said, "It's an emergency please put her on."

To my surprise and relief, he called Pat to the phone. I had to be brief. I simply asked her what time she was leaving. I waited and waited for her. But no sight of her. I was getting frustrated and began questioning the wisdom of hanging around. Then finally, she appeared and simply greeted me with a smile and a brief hello.

I resisted the urge to tell her how long I had been waiting. I merely said, "Let's go," and off we went. I was in good spirits as I took her to her home. Nothing was going to come between us now. However, my enthusiasm had blinded me of some apathy in Pat's demeanour. I didn't sense that her mind was elsewhere.

It didn't take long for her to drop a bombshell. She revealed to me that she was already engaged and had come to London to discuss marriage arrangements. **whoops!**

I was somewhat annoyed and disappointed that she should wait until now to tell me. So, I made my way home. Once my mixed emotions had settled, I decided to visit her again. I wanted to ask her what the situation was between us. Her comments had been ambiguous, and I needed clarity. A mobile phone in those days would have saved a lot of time.

So, without notice, I called at her house on a Saturday. I was shocked to see her fiancé, Brian. was already there. **Another Whoops!**

That made things just a wee bit awkward. What do I say? How am I going to handle this situation? She then introduced me to Brian. I was speechless and wanted to crawl into a hole. What do I say?

I mentally kicked myself, and thought, "What am I doing here? Why on earth did I toss that coin? What a mess it's got me into!"

Then Brian turned toward me and smiled. He then reached out to shake my hand and said, "I wish you all the best with Pat".

Did I hear right? I wanted to say something appropriate. But somehow the words couldn't come out. I had a tremendous feeling of respect and empathy for Brian and for what he was going through.

He must have been distraught. Firstly, by the loss of his fiancé and secondly, by the cruel way it was achieved. I wanted to wish him well, but somehow words wouldn't heal his pain.

My thoughts were now turning over rapidly. I mentally considered the new situation. My mind reverted to that evening when I resorted to tossing a coin.

A thought flashed across my mind...

One toss of a coin had determined my destiny!

Not only mine but others too. I would not have come to Australia without Pat, I would not have many children, grandchildren, or great-grandchildren. And I never had the slightest inkling of the huge global implications and human lives impacted by that tossed coin. This memoir seeks to explore the far-reaching implications of that fateful decision.

CHAPTER 2

Where it All Started

A mid the thunderous blitz of Nazi bombs tearing through London's streets like a relentless storm, I drew my first breath in 1942. Our once bustling neighbourhood now lay in ruins, every third house reduced to rubble by the merciless fury of war.

But it wasn't just buildings that crumbled; It was families too. Within my family, a single bomb had taken the lives of two parents and three innocent children, leaving behind a gaping void that would haunt me for years to come.

In the aftermath of the war's fury, my family were housed in a temporary prefabricated home. Necessities of life were only available by way of ration coupons which severely restricted access to items such as bread, milk, eggs, and other essentials. I saved original ration coupons from the immediate war period and have attached them below.

Actual post war coupons

It was several years before toilet rolls were introduced.

In every street there was a pig bin where all uneaten food was placed. It is interesting to note that this concept of recycling waste foodstuffs is now being implemented throughout Australia. It was a time of deprivation, where even the simplest pleasures were luxuries beyond reach. And how much more did we appreciate the daily necessities when rationing was lifted?

I remember the joy of eating a slice of bread, unashamedly covered with a huge helping of jam. But nothing could indulge our tastebuds like the delight of a Mars bar. So sad we now take such luxuries for granted. However, these pleasures were short-lived. Amid my newfound freedom, I suffered a barrage of diseases which included measles, chickenpox, tonsillitis, mumps, and following all the other diseases, I incurred the killer of many a child, the dreaded scarlet fever.

I remember an ambulance calling at our home. I was quite excited and called my mum, "There's an ambulance outside our house." I never had a clue what they were doing there. They knocked at the door and got me to lie on a stretcher. This was exciting. They took me to a hospital where I was placed in an isolation unit. I still didn't know what it was all about.

I remained in the ward for 5-6 weeks. I remember that a younger lad of about 6 years old was brought into the ward but was well separated from me. The only thing I can remember was that one morning, the lad opposite called out to me, "Can you please wipe my bottom" I was horrified but performed the task like a professional.

This was 1950. A few months after my release from hospital, life was back to normal. But one night at about 2am, I heard feet quietly shuffling outside my bedroom room. It was a burglar! I was shaking with fear and called out, "Who's there?" It went silent. Then very quietly, my door slowly closed. I hid under the bed clothes not daring to look up. After a short while I tentatively peeked over my bedclothes and saw the door was now open again. Next morning when I told my dad about the burglar, he said I must have been dreaming. Later in the morning my dad noticed in the hall the electricity meter box filled with coins, had been wrenched away from the wall and all the money stolen. From that time on, every time there was a creaking floor or similar noise, I just froze under the bedclothes until it was gone.

Our house was only six homes away from the Saint Andrews Church where I would attend Sunday School. On Saturday, it was a tradition that the Sunday School boys play football against other teams at the local park. We were quite good. But not as good as our predecessors from the Sunday School. They were so good that they joined a small local league and the club's name was St Andrews Sunday School Football Club. As it was in the Fulham district, the name was later changed to Fulham Football Club. They are now in the Premier league in England. (Read the club's history.) I'm proud to be part of the club's heritage. I'm unaware of any other Sunday School in the world rising to such heights.

It will be seen later in this manuscript, that I seem to be the target of cheating or foul play. In my last day at school, I watched some boys larking around, and begin to burn a school jacket to celebrate it being the last day. I stood watching until the fire started. Not wishing to get involved, I walked over to the other side of the school to get as far from the fire as possible. The guilty lads were taken to the headmaster and were expelled from school. The headmaster then called me into his office and said another lad witnessed me causing the fire. I denied it. But he insisted and made me stand in his office until I confessed. When it was time to go home, the headmaster said, "we need to finalise the matter. Just say you were involved, and I promise we shall forget the whole matter. You can then go home."

Foolishly I believed him. I said, "OK, I done it" He then said, "I knew you were involved. You're suspended!"

He went completely against his word. I learnt an important lesson in life. I should have stood by the truth.

When I left school, I needed to earn some money, so I took on a job with the Telfer's Meat Pie factory. It was not automated like today. One floor had the huge freezer where the meat was stored and butchered. I believe the bottom floor consisted of the packing and distribution and Admin.

Where I worked, there was one very long conveyor belt which had people positioned on both sides of the moving conveyor belt. It started off with raw ingredients and pastry and ended up as a pie ready for placing in the oven. Each person had their own responsibility.

On my first day I had a fork and had to stab each pie three times as it passed me. Not exactly a skilled function. It was so boring that after three days of stabbing pies, I was moved on along with others on the belt.

My next job was to pick up three pies at a time as they passed by on the conveyor belt. I held one pie in each hand, and one supported in the middle. I had to put the three pies on to a tray on the other side and when the trolley was full, another person who was standing there all day, would unload the trolley on to an elevator in the wall where it went down to the oven for cooking. I went home dreaming of pies. The various duties were rostered around every few days as they were so monotonous. There were no seats, so we all stood in the same spot all day.

Notwithstanding the soul-destroying duties along the conveyor belt, many of the ladies had worked on the belt for numerous years. They were always cheerful and hardworking. I couldn't endure working in the pie factory for long, so I left it to join a travelling fair ground. I was only 14, but tall and strong. It was hard work, but I loved the atmosphere.

My primary job was to assist in the construction of a roundabout until it was complete. I then had to collect the money. To save time, the boss started the roundabout before all the money had been collected. This meant collecting the money whilst the roundabout had started. And it spun round at a frightening speed, up and down and shaking and vibrating. I could barely stand up, let alone collecting money. This was the first and only time I have ever been sacked.

So, I applied to join a bank and started on 10 August 1958. What a transition! Meat pies, fair ground and now banking. From jeans and tee shirt to charcoal grey or pin striped suits, or similar. White shirt and tie were obligatory. But this became more relaxed in only a matter of a few years due to the easing of trends in the 50s. We addressed the manager and some senior staff as sir or Mr Smith. The manager and some senior staff wore a bowler hat. I loved banking and was good at it.

CHAPTER 3

Spreading our Wings

The Innocence of Youth

I was raised in a boy's school and as mentioned earlier, I had no dealings or experience with girls. It's hard to believe that, at no time, either in Primary, Junior, or High school, were we ever taught the facts of life. And we certainly never had the internet to fill us in on the gaps.

For example, when I was aged 11, one of our teachers was appointed to sit on the jury of a rape case. I asked a friend, "What is rape?" he responded, "It's the birds and the bees with force." Not wishing to show my ignorance, I nodded my head knowingly, and said, "Yes, of course," What the hell was he talking about? 'Birds and bees???"

Determined to boost our knowledge about the opposite sex, my mate Mick and I went to a bingo session in which we decided that if either of us won we would share the proceeds and visit a shady strip club in London's Soho district. (Although I was only aged 13, I was 6'4" tall. Mick also looked old for his age). Just for the record and to demonstrate how sharp my memory is, the songs that were being played at the club were: Dark Town Strutters Ball and Chattanooga Choo Choo

We felt like naughty boys playing truant at school. All we wanted was a glimpse of what was missing in our sexual education. How disappointed we were! The performance was very modest. Girls regularly wear far less on any beach nowadays. It's also probably another reason why no one stopped us going in.

More importantly, our voyeurism never did reveal what made a girl different from a boy until we reached further into our teens. Shame on the schools and the teachers for neglecting this important subject.

A most amazing party that is etched in my memory

Just two years after our strip club visits, Mick and I became more adventurous. It was getting close to Christmas, and Mick and I had just enjoyed an evening at a local pub. We were in a merry mood as we walked home. It wasn't long before we could hear what sounded like Calypso music. This aroused our interest. We were always ready to gate-crash a party and partake in some free drink.

We found the house with the music and noted that the front door was left open. This was going to be easy. I devised a tactic that would allow us to enter the home without being recognised. We would simply walk in backwards and people would think we were leaving. Big mistake. The host saw through our little ruse.

"Come in!" boomed a loud voice from the lounge. We turned around and saw a huge black African. We were momentarily terrified. He put our minds at ease and introduced himself as the High Commissioner for Ghana. He then continued with the good part, "This is my wife, she'd love you to dance with her. But first, allow me to get you some drinks". "Pinch me I'm dreaming" I was saying to myself. Attractive ladies and lots of drink! Mick looked at me. I could tell he was thinking the same thing. I guess the High Commissioner was required to be hospitable to the locals. And we were happy to oblige.

We drank heartily. We could never afford anything more than the usual few pints of beer in pubs. The room was filled with many guests. All black except us two. I suspected most were from Africa. The music was lively, drinks flowed freely, and everyone was friendly.

I recall dancing several times with a slim black lady (his wife?) and drinking a variety of cocktails. And that is all I can remember! I was away with the fairies! No doubt we would certainly have drunk the cocktails and spirits with a totally carefree spirit, causing us to be still further inebriated. I'm assuming we made our own way home that night.

I'm confident we paid the appropriate price the next day for the previous night's excesses, in terms of remorse and heavy heads. It was an extraordinary party. One of the best I've attended. And how many people have attended a party hosted by the High Commissioner for Ghana and danced with his wife?

CHAPTER 4

Settling In

The trials and tribulations of married Life

When Brian had bid Pat and I farewell, it was only a matter of weeks before we got engaged. We decided to celebrate our engagement by going to see a live performance of the Everley Brothers at a city theatre. Their support group were four young fresh-faced lads who called them selves the Rolling Stones. I wondered if we would ever hear them again. Just a couple of months later we got married and spent our honeymoon on the Island of Jersey. With marriage came responsibility and domesticity.

Our humble bedsitter was in the suburb of Brixton which was predominantly West Indian. (year 1964). Amidst the chaos of our cramped quarters, the chiming of bells from the church next door blended with the rousing laughter from the pub across the road. I enjoyed watching the West Indian families going to church. The small girls wore colourful, flared dresses and petticoats, and the boys wore smart suits with bow ties. From our house, I could hear the joyful singing and shouts of Amen!

But it was in that environment Pat and I struggled to find our footing. Living in one room is hard enough at the best of times. Especially, as Pat and I were still adjusting to living together after living separately until then. It put an immense strain on our relationship. Pat worked at the House of Commons and regularly got home at 2am and woke me in the process. There must be better times to make love!

My Hilarious Saga of Outsmarting the Local Council (1968)

How satisfying it is to overcome the red tape of a local council disposal service! It all started innocently enough. We had a new lounge suite on its way and needed to rid ourselves of the old one. This should have been a simple matter. Just call up the council and have them haul it away.

But the council does things differently. It agreed to collect the lounge suite but refused to take my old motorbike. Well, that simply wasn't good enough. If they wouldn't take the bike, I'd just have to get a bit creative.

And so, I devised a scheme to outsmart the council in the most ingenious way possible. First, I carefully unstitched the seams of the lounge suite, removing every bit of stuffing until it resembled a sad, deflated balloon.

Now for the bike. I buried the mainframe of the bike in some wasteland. I then disassembled the engine, saddle, handlebars, and wheels. Next, I snugly fitted them into the base of the settee. It was now time to carefully place all the nuts, bolts, chains, and other miscellanea etc. into every available space.

There was nothing left of the motorbike. It was completely housed within the confines of one settee. Even the most seasoned mechanic would raise an eyebrow at my plan to place the bike into its final resting place. A few expertly placed stitches later, and the deed was done! The bike had vanished into the depths of upholstery.

Now came the moment of truth – the council truck's arrival. As the unsuspecting driver approached, I couldn't help but stifle a chuckle. He thought he was in for a routine pickup, but little did he know he was about to become a player in a comedy of errors.

As he attempted to lift the deceptively heavy lounge suite, I offered my assistance, feigning innocence. With a smug grin, I took hold of one end while the driver struggled with the other.

And then it happened! My side soared skyward, whilst the other end, heavy with a clattering of bike parts fell onto the poor driver's lap.

Struggling to keep a straight face, I watched the driver sprawled beneath the unruly settee. He then made the most hilarious of comments, "They don't make them like this anymore!"

Eventually, we managed to wrangle the bloated settee onto the truck. At that point, I couldn't resist probing the driver about their disposal methods.

He responded that they leave the settee at the tip's entrance to be taken away by any young couple hoping to get something for nothing. I couldn't help but smile at the thought of some family member unwittingly perched upon a makeshift throne of motorbike components.

And amidst the chaos, my wife Pat – the silent witness to my madcap scheme, lurked in the shadows, too embarrassed to show her face. Looking back, I'm amazed that I would go to such lengths to outsmart the council.

But I'd do it again if I had to.

Swingers abound.

We bought our first house in a small group of about 80 new homes built alongside a charming village in Kent called Hoo St Werburgh. We were young couples, and one would expect we would go about business devoting our times to our houses and gardens. Not so!

According to Pat who always had her ear to the ground, wife-swapping was rife just four houses up from our house. Three families on our side of the road, swapped regularly with three families on the opposite side. However, one of those families ended up swapping for good.

I kept away from these activities, until one night I was invited to a friendly game of cards whilst my wife Pat was at work as a barmaid. There were three men, including myself, and three women. I guess one of the husbands was at work and I was chosen to be the stand in. I agreed and when I sat down, I was advised that we were playing strip poker, and the winner was the only one still wearing some clothing. "Now they tell me" I thought. The game got to the stage where only I and one of the wives were left with clothes on.

Those who lost their clothes bowed out without any embarrassment or shame; They had been sleeping with one another, so it was no big deal. I was still playing, modestly dressed in my underpants, and the remaining wife was left wearing very skimpy panties. Her brief underwear should have aroused my suspicions about her intentions after the game. Furthermore, the game only lasted 15-20 minutes. I wondered "Is this really what we've all gathered here for, just a short game of cards?' I was getting increasingly concerned that this strip poker would, in due course, be a pre-cursor for a "sexual orgy" for all the participants.

It was now my turn of a card and my reputation, and my modesty rested on the turning of one card. (Not unlike tossing a coin, I mused) My sole opponent left in the game seemed quite unabashed at being in a state of undress, even though her husband was there.

It will be recalled that as a lad I visited a strip tease in London's Soho district. In this game, I was not only watching a strip tease, but I was also a part of it! There were three men including myself, and three ladies. I thought, "The longer I stay around, the harder it will be to extradite myself. I wanted to get out NOW!

I took a long and exaggerated look at my watch as a hint that I would be looking for an excuse to politely slip out. But they weren't going to buy that one. You don't walk away from a card game especially at this stage. I thought of Pat coming home and seeing me in this state of undress. I would have a lot of explaining to do, I panicked and slithered out like a lizard about to be trod on. I decided I couldn't stay for just one more turn of the card. And I certainly didn't want to flash my goods to other men's wives. I never did find out what happened after I left.

They were determined to continue for the rest of the night and I'm sure my absence would not be a problem to such sexually active and resourceful people.

I needn't have been concerned about Pat being upset about my involvement in the card game. When I told her, she thought it was funny. I didn't get any more invitations to our street's extra-curricular activities. In fact, I never heard from them again.

And then there were three

I remember the day when Pat gave birth to her first baby. She was taken to the hospital in Chatham, Kent as a precaution. The ward never had modern items such as I Pads, Head phones, sanitary pads, mobile phone, TV etc.

I drove my motor bike to the hospital to visit her and arrived late due to an accident I had on my bike on the way. I called into the ward and apologised for my blood covered face. The conversation went as follows:

Pat: "What have you been up to?"

Me: "I had a small fall on my bike."

Pat: "You'd better get that washed off."

Me: "Yeah, I'll do it when I get home. How are you feeling? Any news of the baby?"

Pat: "Oh Yes, I've had the baby."

Me: "Well done! What was it?"

Pat: "It is a girl." (I presume I would have given her a kiss – I was too excited to remember such details.)

"You can go and see her if you want."

I then went into the special ward with incubators for premature births and was amazed at how small the baby was. (Note I was still using the term, 'baby' instead of 'girl'.)

I can't remember how Pat came home. I never had a car and didn't know anyone who did. That question will remain a mystery.

Nowadays, we know the gender of the baby long before it is born, and we certainly never had all the ceremonies and parties as they have now. We also have prenatal classes for mum and dad.

And for the record, the baby mentioned above is my daughter, Janet, who is now 56 years old and has children and grandchildren of her own.

CHAPTER 5

Australia Beckons (1969)

The Big Move

Whilst my pay in a London bank was modest, the huge fares and ninety minutes of commuting to and from the city were a huge strain.

I applied for a job with the London head office of the Commonwealth Bank. When the interviewer heard my plight, he said, "Why don't you go to Australia?

When I got home, it took just half an hour for me to declare, "Why not?"

I put the proposition to my wife, Pat. And within a matter of minutes, we had made up our minds. "Yes, let's go," we declared in unison. So, we proceeded to Australia House the very next day to complete the application form.

Is this a world record?

But little did we know the full extent and implications of our decision. And we had no idea of what we were letting ourselves in for.

Life at Sea

We travelled as a family. My two parents, sister Barbara, daughter Janet who was just three years old, and son Daniel, who was still a baby.

We travelled on a Greek ship called the Ellinis, which was crammed full of migrants. I shared a small cabin with a single man.

My diary states the ship docked at Los Palmas on May 18, 1970. Being on holiday mode, we took the opportunity to shop and savour some excellent local beer. Time slipped away from us, and to our horror, we suddenly realised we were cutting it close to our ship's departure time.

There was a loud yell, "Hey! We've got to run...fast! We're going to miss the ship!"

We sprinted back, juggling a toddler and a baby. The ship's horn sounded very close by. As we neared, ropes were being untied. Desperately, we yelled, "Wait for us!"

Exhausted but relieved, we made it onboard just before the gates shut. We quickly stowed our shopping in our cabins and headed to dinner. Later that evening, we enjoyed the onboard entertainment. The singer's favourite song was Neil Diamond's "Sweet Caroline" which he sang each night. Remarkably, the song remains popular worldwide six decades later.

On May 28, 1970, we arrived in Cape Town and were confronted with the stark reality of racial segregation and apartheid. Whites and blacks were kept separate; There were long queues of black people at government offices like post offices and only one or two white people were in the queue at the same building. It wasn't until May 1990 that negotiations to end segregation commenced,

Fremantle Looms in the Distance

As we rested peacefully on the deck, an excited cry pierced the tranquillity.

'I can see land! I can see land!"

Within minutes, everyone rushed to the port side of the ship in eager anticipation, as they watched the captain expertly manoeuvre the ship towards the Fremantle port. It was hard to believe that we finally made it after four long weeks of being couped up on the ship! As we walked the gangway from the ship to shore, there was a collective thrill surging through our hearts.

"We've made it. We really have made it!"

The Australian government had initiated a "Populate or Perish" policy, to be achieved by mass immigration. And as a result, the ship's passengers expected a warm welcome.

How wrong we were! Our welcome was far from warm.

Upon disembarking, a tall man in an unbadged Khaki uniform directed us into a hall designated for migrants. His manner was brusque as he shouted instructions.

We were then herded into a larger hall, where he outlined the house rules.

Summoning my family to one side. He informed us abruptly that the Australian Government hadn't received our entry papers. Consequently, we couldn't stay in Australia. Too stunned to protest vigorously, we agreed to meet the manager the next day.

After a restless night, we approached the manager's office, ready to argue our case. A balding, stout man greeted us warmly, shaking our hands with a friendly smile. We started to raise the issue of the missing papers. But he waved his hand, and said, "Don't worry about that. I've taken care of it with our London office." I was taken aback by his comment and thought that perhaps they really do want us after all.

He then distributed some road maps, information booklets, bus timetables etc. The manager then invited us to call in on him if we had any problems. We left his office with a new sense of purpose.

CHAPTER 6

A New Life – A New Hope

Heaven on Earth

I t was hard to believe that in England, it took ninety minutes each way to commute to and from work, leaving me with hardly anything from my wages after fares.

But from my very first day in Australia, I walked to work and doubled my pay. This was too good to be true.

The Australian culture is very different from England's. Many migrants returned to their home countries where they felt more comfortable. We made a vow never to use the expression, "Back home." Australia was our home. We rejected invitations to join various British clubs where much talk centred around the 'Old Country'.

Our family wasted no time signing up to become Australian citizens. We might have an English accent, and we might be referred to as Poms, but we saw ourselves as Dinki Di Aussies.

Emigrating was a significant risk. We left home and family behind. We put up with substantial changes in the new environment, even if there was some mild ribbing. It required a resilient spirit. And like cream, we rose to the top. And we soon got valued and appreciated.

It didn't take long to participate in the local culture. Each morning, before work, we went to the beach for a run, and to surf the waves. Compare that with the ninety-minute train commute every day in England!

The Osborne Park branch where I worked had a large contingent of Italians and Yugoslavs. Such lovely people, all from immigrant families themselves. They made it so easy to settle in in the early days.

It wasn't long before I was appointed as a bank manager at several branches. One day whilst managing the branch at Cottesloe in 1983 (one of Perth's most popular beaches) an Indian gentleman named Mr Sharma, called in to open an account.

We got talking and Mr Sharma was interested to learn that I also had a separate business with a partner. He then went on to ask me, "Would you and your partner together with your wives do me the honour of joining my wife and me for dinner one evening? This was too good to refuse. I agreed without hesitation.

We dressed in our finest evening wear and waited to be shown our places by an attentive waiter. Once seated, the wine waiter took orders for cocktails, wines, and a fine port to conclude the evening's banquet.

Mr Sharma then requested an assortment of bowls filled with sumptuous Indian dishes to be brought to our table. As we enjoyed the meal, more dishes continued to arrive. These were accompanied by some of the best local wines.

We concluded the evening with a vintage Tawny Port.

We then indicated to Mr Sharma that we thoroughly enjoyed the most delectable meal and accompanying drinks. We were now ready to go.

He then signalled for the bill. The waiter promptly brought it to us. Mr Sharma turned to my partner and me and declared, "Gentleman, I want to thank you both very much for your wonderful generosity."

He and his wife then stood and bowed. They then departed the restaurant quietly and swiftly with the bill unpaid! We looked at each other for a few minutes with eyebrows raised and mouths wide open. We were speechless and dumbfounded. I reached into my wallet and settled the bill somewhat grudgingly, not wishing to make a scene.

My partner and I then departed the restaurant with a dazed look on our faces. As we stood outside, neither of us could utter a word. We just looked at each other in total silence. Then spontaneously, we burst into uncontrollable laughter. We had been outsmarted... by a brazen scammer. It was a brilliant masterstroke, smoothly executed.

We laughed all the way home. We were still laughing the next morning when we held a post-mortem. We never did see Mr Sharma again. Not surprisingly. You had to admire the gumption and audacity of Mr Sharma. I wonder how many other people received the same treatment.

Looking for Greener Pastures

I moved up the ladder of the Bank at the local, international, and senior levels. However, banking was undergoing huge change, and bank managers no longer had the status and income that they previously enjoyed. It was time to move on.

I was open to offers of a good income and prospects of overseas travel. It wasn't long before I received an opportunity which met these criteria. The timing (1985) was perfect. Looking back, it was too good to be true. But I should have taken note of the warning signs.

My children were now adults or in their late teens. They were no longer dependent upon me for their financial well-being.

CHAPTER 7

Flying High

Let's now look at those early days

The 80s was a time of excitement in the financial world. Banks were lending extravagantly. Local highflyers like Alan Bond, Laurie Connel and Christopher Skase were building their empires. Money was freely available.

As the winds of change swept through the financial world, I found myself caught up in the exhilarating whirlwind of opportunity that followed in its wake. Everyone was jumping on the gravy train. The world was in a spin.

It was in this environment that I took up an offer from a project management firm to join their team to promote a select range of products to international organisations that had indicated a positive interest. It was with some trepidation that we set off. We prepared ourselves for triumphs and exhilaration. But in the end, all we got was tribulations and adversity.

In normal circumstances, my conservative banking experience would exert influence on the situation. But this was no ordinary situation. It was an uncontrollable tsunami that was approaching at a frightening pace.

We set off from Perth and had a short stopover in India. (1986) Our reservation was at the iconic Taj Mahal Hotel in Mumbai.

We stood outside the airport looking for a taxi. I waved one down and went to pick up my suitcase containing all my belongings. It had vanished...stolen in an instant.

I no longer had any clothes; except those I was wearing. However, my waistbelt containing documents and money remained safe around my waist. So, I immediately left it at the hotel reception.

Somewhat dazed at this turn of events, I went for a short walk around the local markets. I didn't see my partner until dinner time. It was not long before my shirt clung to me from the walking and humidity. I took one look at the cool sparkling hotel swimming pool.

I was completely on my own, and could not resist jumping in. My suitcase had been stolen and I had no other clothes, so I stripped off the clothes I was wearing and jumped into the pool with gay abandon.

I can't remember what I wore in the pool. It was quite likely my underpants, as my suitcase had been stolen.

But I do remember quite clearly that it was only a matter of a few minutes when I noticed that my remaining clothes, which I had left alongside the pool, had now also disappeared. No doubt stolen.

Embarrassed, annoyed, soaking wet, and almost naked, I was rescued by a sympathetic member of the staff who gave me a loose fitting traditional Indian gown which was amazingly cool. I only needed it until the following day when I could buy something more appropriate.

Relating this situation in future years aroused much laughter. But it wasn't funny at the time. I was alone in a noisy, crowded country of mixed cultures. I was angry and grew somewhat distrustful of everybody.

Anyway, we had a successful business meeting in Mumbai (1986). My mind was now focused on my meeting in Dallas the next day. And my immediate task would be to buy some new clothes. I was fully insured and went straight to the first men's clothing shop I saw.

I just love seeing a high-performing sales professional in full flight demonstrating his stock. And this man from Dallas was the best. I was more bedazzled by his sales technique than I was by his wares. I was totally in awe of his presentation. It was sheer magic and great entertainment.

As a result, I came away with a suitcase filled with far more stock than I had originally intended to buy.

I sent a card from Dallas on 6 July 1986, which said we had "a good time on 4th and were treated to good US hospitality. The men really do wear tall hats and cowboy shirts."(I probably should have also written cowboy boots)

Once our business was completed in Dallas, we set off to New York.

There's not much I can say about New York. I sent a card home to the family on 16 July 1986. I wrote, "I've had enough of New York. Cars blow their horns continuously for no reason, drivers are rude, and so are shopkeepers…never a please or thank you, change plonked on to the counter, etc".

It's fast, exciting, rude, noisy, massive helpings of food, with huge dollops of cream. It was an amazing experience to go out at 2 am and find the street filled with taxis and other traffic. I wondered, "Where are they all going?"

I skilfully weaved my way through the never-ending flow of traffic to the other side of the road and proceeded to the nearest burger bar. I smiled to myself that I didn't need to look, as I could smell my way there.

I ordered the most enormous burger I have ever seen. I jokingly thought, "It looks like a Volkswagen Beetle...and nearly as big!!"

As I strolled along the Avenue window shopping, I was amazed that everything was within short walking distance.

During our stay in New York, we attended a business meeting 200 miles north. We opted for a chauffeur-driven limousine, complete with luxurious amenities and a well-stocked minibar. We reclined in the plush seats, enjoying the ride in comfort. Upon our return, we warmly thanked our courteous driver, exchanged warm farewells, and headed off into the bustling crowd.

Our journey spanned over 400 miles. However, there was a horrendous oversight...

The driver neglected to collect the fare, which would have been substantial given the distance. We were unable to contact him and therefore unable to settle the bill. We felt bad about his loss. But I'm sure he felt a good deal worse.

On Sunday morning 13th July 1986, I decided to pay a visit to a local church. There was no Google in those days, only Yellow Pages. I selected one at random out of a choice of hundreds. It was called Assembly of God, Harlem

I knew nothing about the area of Harlem. Upon arriving, I observed that the location was significantly dilapidated, with apartments full of broken windows and uncollected garbage. I could not imagine a city like New York having such a run-down location. However, that was 38 years ago. I understand that Harlem is currently experiencing a new renaissance.

The best words to describe the church were very vocal, happy, and friendly. The people greeted me warmly. I sensed they weren't accustomed to white visitors. The service started very early and continued for many hours without a break and appeared to finish well into the evening. People simply paused to have some lunch and then resumed the service.

I was amused when it was the time to take up a financial offering. The congregation consisted mainly of working class, low paid people. They were not wealthy like the average New Yorker. Yet they stood in a line along the aisles facing the front and sang in unison a repetitive chorus with a prominent beat, as follows: "We are going… to give our dues, we are going … to give our dues… etc" The singing harmonised with what looked like tribal steps performed in with a syncopated beat, 12…123…12…123. I was mesmerised. I didn't participate.

Out of curiosity, I searched for this church recently (2024) on YouTube and was amazed to discover that outside the building were long queues of tourists. Presumably, bus loads include the church as part of their itinerary. The church building must incorporate a gallery for tourists.

With New York behind me I was now spending more time in the air than on land visiting cities around America, Canada, and Mexico. This itinerary included Salt Lake City. Vancouver, San Diego, and Mexico.

One thing that amazed me was that the plane provided a phone for each passenger, conveniently situated under the armrest for easy access. I was not aware that this technology was available in those days (1987). Happily, I was able to ring through to reschedule our business meeting.

Meanwhile, evcryone was recklessly riding the gravy train, spending big and having no regard for the consequences.

Then it happened when everyone thought it would all go on forever… **the bubble burst in 1988.**

The highflyers came down with a thud. Billions of dollars in savings and investments wiped out overnight. It was not just the highflyers who were impacted. The Western Australian government including its Premier Brian Burke also fell unceremoniously (Mid 1980's).

Then all the king's horses and all the king's men….

We then made our way home via London, where I made a short stop to catch up with friends and relatives.

Travelling all over the world took a toll on my life. It sounds like lots of fun and a good holiday. No such thing.

My wife and children were back in Australia. I missed them very much. Particularly, the children, who were really adults. I aimed to set them up for life, but taxation and other costs eroded that dream.

CHAPTER 8

Down but Not Out

The high-flyers had come home to roost, and now I had joined the ranks of the unemployed.

I was an athlete in my younger days. We used to say that the measure of a person's fitness is not how *fast* he/she runs, nor how *far* he/she runs, it is measured by **how quickly he/she recovers.** I was down but not out. I wasn't going to sit around licking my wounds. My resolve was being tested to the extreme. Again, I asked myself:

> *Where is the man who spent over an hour searching through the Yellow Pages to locate his girlfriend's place of occupation?*

Where is the man who travelled halfway across the globe to Australia, overcoming all obstacles to set up a new life?

Was not the toss of the coin a toss of destiny? In my heart, I believed it was.

Note how I look for my previous successes to determine my decisions, and my decisions to determine my destiny.

It *was time to take stock*, to pick myself up and refocus my vision. I believe that there is a spiritual dimension from which we can draw strength. I'm not religious but I'm confident that if I trust Jesus to be a source of inspiration and strength, I would be a new person.

It didn't take long for me to forget the past ups and downs. I was already looking forward to some new challenge.

CHAPTER 9

Making it in the Real World

Travel for the Disabled

Back home (1987), it didn't take long to find work and I became General Manager of a travel agency for disabled persons I looked after the finance and the business development. Not the sales.

One day, a man was standing in the reception for some while, and no one was available to help him. I couldn't watch him wait any longer. I stood up and asked if I could help. He gave me his name, and said he ran an organisation for boys in their early teens and was looking for a holiday for the group. I knew from my records that we had a group tour for Singapore recently cancelled. It was just what he wanted, and I signed him up.

When he left, I proudly told Jean, the sales manager, of my success and informed her of the man's name. She shrieked, ***"You've just sold a 'Sightseeing tour of Singapore to a group of blind boys!"***

It was time to put our heads together: My creativity and Jean's resourcefulness. Jean said, "Don't despair, we'll give them the best tour they've ever had. We'll take them to the food markets where they can smell and taste all the wonderful delicacies. We'll then take them to the animal farm where they will hug and stroke the animals. There'll be pillion riding of motorbikes and a range of other activities".

And we did. They had the holiday of a lifetime. The sightseeing tour of Singapore became a regular feature, not just for this blind organisation, but also for others. We just changed the name of the tour.

It's a fact that people with good eyesight don't utilise all their senses like those who are short-sighted. Jean and I travelled the nation offering our specialised services to disabled organisations nationwide. The business took off as sales soared. Within six months we were approached by Jetset (now HelloWorld) who wanted to take over the company's business with its disability emphasis. We gladly accepted their offer.

The Thrill of Selling Businesses

I progressed from there to becoming a business broker in 1990. I loved the challenge of selling businesses and made very good money. But it wasn't easy and not for everybody. On my first day, I was directed to an empty desk and enquired, "Where are the businesses I have to sell?" I was told, "You don't have any. You must go and get them. That means knocking on doors. Alternatively, sell someone else's businesses that are too hard to sell".

Looking at my empty table, I once again had to draw on the same determination that empowered me many years ago when flicking through hundreds of Yellow Pages to find a waitress. Just thinking about past victories gave me the single-mindedness to press on. Didn't the tossed coin determine my destiny? I had to believe it. If it came up tails, I wouldn't be here.

Within a matter of days, I sold an "Underground Drilling Business." I never had a clue what that was! Nor did anyone else. And I thought" If I can sell that. I can sell anything." Whilst I made good money selling businesses. It wasn't my only motivation. I loved "The Thrill of the Chase." In short, I loved what I was doing. I enjoyed helping people make successful businesses out of the ones I sold to them. My philosophy aligns with Zig Ziglar who said, "You can have everything in life that you want if you just give enough other people what they want".

Just when things were going well, after five years of selling businesses, the country was hit with a major recession and the market went completely dead. Business Broking was the most satisfying and happiest time of my business life. I was very successful and enjoyed every minute of it. Pat was happy with my flexible and short working hours. Not for the first time I was without an income. You will see in this memoir that I often undertook activities which were fully funded by myself. i.e. I received no income. These included: the Aboriginal Program, the Indonesian Mission, China, plus ten years of nursing my wife. I always landed on my feet. Please note that I am not proposing that other people follow me or do some of the crazy things that I do. My life is unique. I wouldn't wish it on any others. And that is why I am writing this Memoir.

CHAPTER 10

Life in an Aboriginal Community

WARNING: Aboriginal and Torres Straight
Islander readers are warned that the following
chapter and subsequent related photographs
may contain images of deceased persons.

I n 1995, my wife, Pat, and I sought a meaningful
challenge that would make a positive impact on
the lives of others. We decided to immerse ourselves
in an Aboriginal Community (named Gooniyandi) in
Fitzroy Crossing, in the North of Australia.

We knew this choice meant living without a
regular income and embracing a simple lifestyle.
Despite the scorching temperatures, often exceeding
40 degrees Celsius, we settled into a small caravan

alongside the community. Initially, we noticed the community faced challenges. We were informed by one of the missionaries that the public toilet had no paper or soap, just a communal rag. I was pleased to learn that pressure in the right places brought about improvement in this situation and others.

When one of the big trucks accidentally ran over a straying cow, the cow would be brought back and hung up for the community members to slice off a portion. Everyone and everything came to devour the decaying carcass. There were always dogs, flies and likely rats chewing at it before it was brought down, eaten to the bone.

When many of the men reached middle age, i.e. in their 40s, they often deserted their wives for a younger girl of only around 13. As a result, the abandoned wife often became an alcoholic. It was not unusual to see the new wives, who were young teenage girls, holding babies.

I had heard that there was a Witch Doctor in the area and that he elicited fear among some of the locals. They were not specific in what that fear was, and I suspected that they believed he had some magical powers.

I first met the Witch Doctor when I was sitting in the back of a truck. The driver saw a man walking along the road and slowed down. He called out, "Hey Mate, do you want a lift?' The driver, upon identifying the man, turned to me and asked, "You don't mind if we pick up the Witch Doctor, do you? Just move over to allow him to sit down" I nodded my head tentatively. I expected him to ooze some spooky power or aura. But he seemed no different to any other Aboriginal and acknowledged me with a nod.

During my time in the community, I got to know the Witch Doctor on a casual basis. For some strange reason, he attracted the name of Adolf. I'm sure the person who assigned him that name, had no idea of its connotations. He seemed quite a nice man.

It was customary once a year for the Witch Doctor to perform a ritual. This would involve him driving around the community collecting boys who have reached the age of 13 to be circumcised by him in a traditional ceremony. It was a painful and unhygienic procedure taking weeks to heal.

Pat fully absorbed herself in the work, spending most of the day inside the communities. Everyone appreciated her contribution. They adopted her into the community as a family member. This was a very privileged position. She was also given a special

Aboriginal name by way of recognition for her services within the community.

However, it was the children who loved and respected her and followed her everywhere. See photos. She was like the Pied Piper. Children surrounded her whenever she appeared. See Pat surrounded with children (look at arrow).

Pat with kids-see arrow

Outside the local pub, there was a huge pile of beer cans about 12M high. When it was decided to give a 5c reward on every empty beer can, the big pile completely disappeared within just a few days.

Several times a month, we joined the community around a fire. It was a ritual that was a very special time for the local Aboriginals. Our presence there reflected the special place that we held in the community.

A huge pot of boiling water, containing a heaped spoonful of tea, sat securely on the fire. Everyone sat around in a circle, with eyes fixed on the flames, regularly topping up their mugs with the well-brewed beverage. When they were finished, they put their unwashed mugs into a bowl for future use.

I felt uneasy about the lack of hygiene when partaking in that event. But I never considered there could be any negative consequences such as Hepatitis A.

Me with Harry

A local Aboriginal called Harry went everywhere with me. His skin was jet black, his hair unkempt, and tribal cuts marked his body. A permanent smile stretched across his face, revealing a gap where two front teeth had been knocked out during a tribal encounter.

He proudly sat alongside me in my vehicle and guided me to outback communities and water holes. I never went anywhere without him. Harry would look at the clear blue sky, and point upwards and say, "Rain coming later today." He was always right. I could always rely upon Harry to be standing in an agreed spot waiting to be picked up.

Harry was not like some Aboriginals who would go "walkabout". This is a term used to describe the practice of some Aboriginals who disappear for a period. It isn't a matter of concern to those remaining, as they know that those who have gone away for a period will always return to the community.

As I was living in the community, it was acceptable to refer to the men as "blackfellas." They used the expression and were happy for the whitefellas in the community to also use it

We went there primarily to assist a missionary couple, who had been faithfully working in the community for many years. They were instrumental in helping us get involved.

Our objectives in the community were to help the people with health, nutrition, sanitary conditions, alcoholism and petrol sniffing, etc.

The Aboriginals are very spiritual people, and the objective of the missionaries was to tap into this realm by preaching the gospel. However, I didn't believe that the Aboriginals understood much of what was preached to them. I believe that most of the time it was white fella talk and went over their heads.

I also had problems with the control the missionaries exercised over the Aboriginals. For example, they could not visit other communities or buy consumer goods without the approval of the missionary.

Their concern was that the Aboriginals had little Idea of finance and budgeting, and would end up spending a week's income on a TV and have nothing left for food etc. I respected that view but didn't wholly agree.

The alternative argument was that if the Aboriginals had no control over their money they would never learn and never achieve self-determination. In short, they were destined to be continually dependent upon the white fellas.

Even now many years later, the tribal elders have varying views on the above matters. They have a whole lot more wisdom on this subject than I do, so I don't get involved.

Unfortunately, I contracted Hepatitis A after about a year in the community. The disease, together with the extreme heat, and my age were taking a toll on my general health. We aimed to stay much longer but the Hepatitis A knocked me for six. I had to go home to recover.

Strangely, my wife, Pat, escaped the infection. Most of the Aboriginals were immune to the disease as it was common for children to be infected with a mild dose when young.

The disease took around three months for me to make an initial recovery, and a further three months to get back to work. The whole exercise had sapped my strength and energy. I had to face the realisation that I could no longer return to the community when I had recovered.

It is now 25 years since we stayed there, and I would like to think that many of the issues and concerns that we felt whilst there have since been addressed.

I understand that there has been improvement and further enhancement of the conditions through government initiatives. However, I don't believe there is an overnight quick fix.

CHAPTER 11

Indonesian Experience

It was 2000 and I was not back to full strength following my bout of Hepatitis and it took a further year of complete rest from work., I was intrigued when I had a call from an Indonesian called Maynard Winata, who was, (and still is) a prison chaplain. I don't know from where he got my name, but we had a few chats through social media, and on one occasion, he just casually asked, "Why don't you come and visit us. The local villages would be thrilled to see you." I suspected he was also seeking help and support for the prisoners who were primarily political.

Their wives, who had to provide for their families without their husband's support, were in great need. As with the Aboriginals, the life of the Indonesian village communities is one of poverty and deprivation.

Indonesian Street

Overall, they are simple and uneducated. They have the strange idea that the people from Caucasian countries have more wisdom. A trip to Indonesia was the last thing on my agenda. Yet, I had just spent 6 months indoors recovering from the Hepatitis. I was yearning to get out of the house and take on a challenge. Just thinking aloud, I like their food, I like their people, it's a country in which I've never been before. I could do a lot worse.

I can't remember the last time I drew an income. I'd be living on the edge. But I'm intrigued. I'm not the sort to turn away from a challenge. So, (using Australian slang) I murmured to myself. "Oh, stuff it. I'm going."

And just as an aside, one might ask where is Pat in all this? She is drawing an income from looking after students. And shortly after my trip, she went to Indonesia herself, to visit the family of Rianto, one her Indonesian students. That was a story for another time.

Off I went and stayed with a local family in Jakarta, who generously provided me with a bed and food. My first challenge was the type of toilet/bathroom which was apparently quite normal in Asian countries. My host, quite nonchalantly, advised me, "The toilet/bathroom is in there." I entered the room and was horrified to discover it consisted of nothing more than a hole in the ground. I had heard of this before, but never in all my wildest dreams expected to encounter this myself. No one had given me instructions or introduced me to this strange arena.

What on earth must I do? I walked around this hole several times in total disbelief. I think I must have expected something to pop up out of the ground. Perhaps there was a door hidden somewhere which would take me to another room with real facilities. Squatting over a hole wasn't exactly easy. In fact, it was darn hard. Europeans have difficulty squatting for long. You see Asians squatting for hours in the Jakarta Street talking to each other. I can't do this for more than 5 minutes and need to hold on to something. Having completed the task I arose somewhat exhausted with the challenge that this had presented me. I still didn't know how to flush away the remains. Interestingly, I had never considered the problems that Western toilets had presented Asians when visiting me.

The next cultural problem I had to encounter was the live-in servant (pembantu). I watched my host call the servant over and indicated for her to take off his shoe and put on a slipper. That is considered too much effort when you have a servant. If I needed to get something from the bedroom, my host stopped me from standing up and indicated that the servant would get it. It's their culture but it took some getting used to. She had the most cheerful and willing character. The only thing you do on your own is mentioned in the previous paragraph.

This was all very good, but where do I fit in? Maynard encouraged me to just come along and meet some of the people. So off we went. My first call was to a small group of around ten people. I'm aware hat they are emotional but was taken back by their outpouring of tears upon meeting me because no-one from another country had ever visited them before. Then they brought out a tray of traditional food which I gladly received. I joined in whatever they were doing and soon discovered that they looked up to the tall white man. In their eyes, I had special faith, wisdom, experience and had the answer their problems. As they needed work for the men and health for the family, they came to me. Would I say a prayer for them. "Not a problem." And it elicited a further outpouring of tears. "We will always remember you, please come back again. Thank you so much" etc. And so, it went on wherever we went. But why am I here? It didn't take long to find out.

Maynard took me to more small gatherings in makeshift buildings or people's homes. Although there were often only ten people present, they had a pastor or leader to conduct the meeting. Many years ago, I was a bank auditor, and I could sniff out problems like a fox can smell an injured rabbit a mile away. And my nose was now twitching. It didn't take me long to form an opinion. And it concerned me deeply. The Pastors and leaders were placing their people under a huge burden. The people were constantly bombarded with calls to stop sinning. The continuous mantra was" You're all a load of sinners." It was an obsession. The people were put under a massive guilt trip and a fear of divine retribution. There were no words of encouragement,

When the leaders and pastors asked me to speak, they assumed I would deliver a message condemning the people just like they did. I am conscious that it is not ethical, when in another country, to tell them what to do. I decided to take that risk. When I spoke, although the people were there, I was speaking primarily to the pastors and leaders. And I didn't pull any punches.

I took the opportunity to share a message which emphasised love, compassion, caring, sharing, forgiveness etc. It seems so elementary, but they had never heard such a message before. No wonder they wriggled uneasily in their seat. When the guilt is lifted, people will have a smile on their face and joy in their heart. The leaders probably weren't ready to make the change. At least, not immediately. But I believed that I sowed a seed.

I visited many of the small communities in villages, generally encouraging them to love one another and be strong. The people were inundated with needs like those constantly faced by the Aboriginals i.e. poverty, hygiene, nutrition, clean water, poor health etc. They were thrilled to have a tall white man from another country come to visit them. They said no one from overseas had ever visited them. The women wept when they saw me. In their minds, the tall white man had the answers to all their problems which were ever present in their difficult life.

There were many bigamists in the communities, and the men wanted to know which wife they should sleep with at night. I felt the man should sleep with the first woman he married. However, I kept such opinions to myself. They also sought answers to other personal issues. The tall white man would know what to say. I wished I had their confidence. Nevertheless, I spent a lot of time and effort into helping people with their queries. My time in Indonesia was a dangerous period. I was unaware of the friction and ill feelings that existed at that time, between Indonesia and Australia due to the East Timor Crisis. The situation was inflamed when someone had erected a large banner across a busy road promoting the Speaker from Australia and providing the time and place. Imagine my feelings upon seeing the banner which told everyone that I would be speaking at the building, just along the road at a specific time. I would be walking into a danger zone and that afternoon, just minutes before I arrived at the building, someone, thinking that I would be there, threw a bomb at the building. See the two photos, which show the destruction.

Bomb Damage in
Indonesian meeting Place

Bomb Damage Room

I narrowly missed being blown up. Remarkably, the back of the building escaped most of the damage. We had to show that we weren't going to let them feel hat they had achieved a victory. So, we conducted the meeting at the rear. I achieved much satisfaction in encouraging the people in the small villages. I told them not to feel condemned. God loves them just as they are.

I stayed in a home in one of the side streets of Jakarta. I was told that the septic tanks were installed many years ago and leaked badly causing an overflow into ditches in front of houses in our street. The contents of the ditches flowed to a drainage system some distance away. Every time the drain was confronted by a crossroad, it went through a tunnel underneath taking its contents to the other side. The problem was that the tunnel underneath the crossroad regularly got clogged up. So, there was a man with a long pole and something like a brush on the end, which he would then use to clear the blockage. As the blockage consisted of a certain degree of effluent, I couldn't help feeling sorry for this poor man. I asked my host how much he would earn for this job, and he advised that he would earn no more than a bowl of rice. I considered this to be an exaggeration but not too far from the truth.

In the West, if we are unemployed, we either rely on our families or the government to provide enough money for food and other necessities. My host advised me that in Indonesian if you don't work, you don't get fed. So, everyone does something to generate an income. People stand at parking lots at shopping centres guiding the the car to any empty spot. They stand at traffic lights and sing etc.

So, most locals always carry a bowl of loose coins to pay these people for their services. It is considered rude to ignore them and you are likely to get your car scratched if you do. I was head and shoulders taller than most Indonesians, often people wanted to express their thanks by buying me a Batik shirt. But the shirts were far too small and not what I needed after purchasing a suitcase full of shirts in New York! After Christmas, many of my male friends and relatives in Australia surprisingly started wearing Batik shirts. I wonder where they got them from.

CHAPTER 12

In the Funeral Business

As I received no income from either the Aboriginal or Indonesian visits, I needed to pursue an activity that would start bringing in some money, and at the same time help me recharge my batteries. Unbelievably, I achieved these objectives in 2005 by joining Prosser Scott Funerals.

My duties were to do everything for the deceased's family. I collected the body at all hours of the day and night and slid them into the freezer. I masterly applied makeup to the deceased with skills that matched that of an experienced beautician.

When I was new to the industry, I told the manager that I had a problem. I couldn't close the lid without squashing the deceased's nose down. He said, "Just sit on the lid and it will go down. He won't know about it!"

I said, "But I will! And every night when I go to bed I will think of that nose, unkindly pressed down."

One day, I was called to the second floor of an apartment block and found the deceased underneath the table in the kitchen. I gently slid him onto the trolley, pushed down the wheels and wheeled it towards the lift.

When the lift doors opened, I discovered that the lift was not big enough to wheel the trolley in horizontally. So, I strapped the body down and stood the trolley into a vertical position. I was then able to ease the body into the lift standing up.

When we reached the first floor there was a crowd of people waiting to enter the lift. I called out, "Stay there, you won't want to come in here." They ignored my pleas and started crowding into the lift.

When they saw that they were looking face to face with a deceased person, they screamed and couldn't get out of the lift fast enough.

If anyone was looking, they would have detected a small smile on my face.

On one occasion, the hearse that I was driving, broke down at a set of traffic lights. I had just picked up the deceased and was driving the hearse back to the funeral parlour. Inside the hearse was a coffin/casket containing a deceased body.

I rang for a replacement vehicle. It was a typical Perth hot day at around 36 degrees. Not the best temperature to hold a deceased person. My plight aroused considerable attention from onlookers sitting in cars at the lights. The distraction caused the other cars to miss their green light.

People in cars behind blew their horns angrily to tell others to move on when the light turned green. When they saw the hearse themselves, their curiosity got the better of them, and they, in turn, also slowed down to get a good look inside the hearse.

This became quite an attraction. It's not the sort of thing that happens every day. It's a good job that not many people had mobile phones with cameras in those days, or we would never have left the lights.

Some of the frightening moments occurred when the deceased's pacemaker wasn't removed before the body was put into the coffin/casket. Even the most experienced undertaker would get a fright when working on the deceased, they see the body suddenly sit up or just shake their body uncontrollably.

I enjoyed being an undertaker, and, to my surprise, I received many a hug from grateful relatives.

I was happy there, but another big offer came along. I don't know whether it was the huge challenge of travelling across Europe, and then across China that influenced me or just the money. But I'm a survivor and I usually land on my feet.

I was conscious of spending too long away from home so, I prepared as much paperwork as possible beforehand to reduce my time overseas.

CHAPTER 13

China Calling

Whenhen China started freeing up its relationship with the West, it sought funding to develop its industry and economy, particularly oil refineries and major property developments. As it was well known that I had international banking experience, I was approached in 2006 to raise around $860M on behalf of a few large Chinese corporations.

Big money beckoned

I was offered a 1% commission on the funds raised ($8M). The process involved travelling to Zurich to put together a consortium of banks and then travelling to Lichtenstein to finalise the deal.

However, before putting together my proposal to the banks, I needed to call on the organisations who were seeking finance, to prepare business plans, financial projections, collateral etc,

As I went from company to company, up and down China, the respective top executives were my hosts. They needed substantial finance and depended upon me to obtain it for them. So, they looked after me very generously. They were CEOs of big companies. Money was no obstacle. I couldn't speak the language and was happy to be wined and dined at the top restaurants. My interpreter came along for the ride.

One interesting thing I noticed was that the wives of the men gave them contraceptives whenever they went out at night. They obviously expected their husbands to misbehave. I soon got one example of what the men got up to.

We were driven to a building with lights flashing. We were then directed to seats overlooking an area which looked like a stage. On it was a carousel which was moving from right to left. Then suddenly there was a parade of around 40 ladies, one at a time. Each one prominently displayed their best features. I soon got the idea of what was happening. It was up to us to choose a lady for the night. Many would not get any housekeeping money that night as only six would be chosen; one for each man.

They were subject to the control of the organisers and depended wholly upon them for the necessities of life, with no means of escape. In essence, they were slaves. I was in a difficult situation. I could not speak the language. And could not retreat from this despicable performance. The Chinese businessman who was my host was sponsoring the evening.

My interpreter was on my right and selected what was the most attractive lady on display. He asked her if she would give him sex that night. She flatly refused. So, he moved on to the next lady who agreed.

Now my turn. After 54 years of marriage, I was not interested in illicit sex. So, I chose the lady who declined my interpreter, and who happened to be the most beautiful. She spent the evening getting me a large supply of exotic drinks and food. Not surprisingly, I can't remember any more about that night or how I got back to the hotel. I'm sure I enjoyed myself with the strong wines. But there was no sex.

In hindsight, I should have chosen the least attractive girl. Perhaps even two of them if permitted. These impoverished individuals would regularly ride the carousel, never getting chosen, and struggling to survive. My regret is that I could only provide freedom for that night. They will continue as slaves until the next wealthy person selects them.

And now I know why the wives gave their husbands contraceptives. How tolerant!

Now back to work. After extensive negotiation, I was able to put together a consortium of banks in Zurich that would underwrite the funding. I then had to travel to Lichtenstein to obtain Letters of credit for $860M to take back to the Chinese organizations concerned.

Liechtenstein is situated between Switzerland and Austria. It boasts a thriving economy. I'm not sure why Lichtenstein was chosen to coordinate the provision of finance. Perhaps there were taxation implications.

The Head of state is Prince Hans-Adam ll. He lives in Vaduz Castle which is at the top of a small mountain. I decided to hike up the pathway to get a closer look at the castle.

On the way up I encountered miniature stables, housing prize-winning cattle. Each stall showcased ribbons and certificates. I was delighted when the cows approached me affectionately licking my hand as though they were were seeking my friendship.

There was a restaurant opposite my hotel, and I had planned to have beef steak that evening for dinner. But I kept thinking of those beautiful cows and could not bring myself to eat beef at that restaurant. In fact, after that event, I never ate meat for many years.

I made my way to the negotiating table in Lichtenstein on the following morning. I was able to secure the Letters of Credits for the requested sum of $860M without too much trouble. It was quite smooth going as a lot of preparatory work had been completed and submitted before our meeting.

However, the Chinese recipients had little ethics or honour.

They took the Letters of /credit (a letter from a bank guaranteeing payment upon presentation) for $860M back to the Chinese banks to see if they could get a better interest rate. It appears that the interest rate that they were originally offered was not acceptable. So, they used the finance that I obtained for them as a lever to cause the Chinese banks to increase their rate. They, in effect, played one bank against another.

And they succeeded. Which meant that my Letters of credit etc were no longer valid. The whole exercise cost me over $8M in commission (less interpreters' fees). It also cost me a good deal of my time initially in Australia, in the preparation of Business Plans and bank documentation, and then in Europe and China to finalise matters.

Been there - Done That

I now look back on this failed venture philosophically. I travelled all over China from top to bottom, I saw some magnificent sights. I stayed at the top hotels, ate the most expensive meals and drinks, and was the guest of honour at all their mealtimes. No one started to eat until I did. And at every course, they made a toast to me, their special guest! I don't know what they drank but it was well known for its potency.

An interesting event occurred at one of the large factories which I visited when preparing my business plan. Upon arriving, I saw a line of around 30 men standing in line, as soldiers do when on parade waiting for inspection. When I asked what it was all about, I was told it was in my honour. I then had to walk along the line, as an army colonel would when inspecting his soldiers. I'd give an approving nod as I passed each man.

I can't remember if I shook their hands, I don't think so

Called on by a persistent prostitute.

I paid for my plane trips to China. Once there, all expenses were paid for, including internal plane flights.

They even sent a high-class, very beautiful prostitute to my room. I declined her services. I settled for only a nonsexual massage. However, my refusal must have dented her pride.

She was determined to get me to respond to her prompting which was designed to stimulate me. I don't know exactly what she did, but it was powerful.

Upon the conclusion of just one hour, I had to sign her invoice to be given to the businesspeople backing me, an amount of US$2,200 for just one hour (which would be much more at today's values).

Since then, men in Australia said that I was stupid to pass up such an opportunity. Interestingly, the women back home applauded me for refusing.

Upon reflection about the China trip, I lost a high commission, but I had a lifetime experience that many people can only envy.

CHAPTER 14

Loss of my Manhood

Just fourteen years ago, in 2010, I had a PSA check to determine the health of my prostate. It was found that I had an aggressive cancer. It was explained to me that I could lose my sexual capacity but keep my life.

The operation was successful, and I was sent to a Men's Health Centre. Otherwise known as Sex Clinic.

The doctor wanted to know whether I had retained my sexual capacity. He took out two sexually explicit magazines to take home to read together with two different coloured pills to be taken on two different nights. I accepted the pills but declined the magazines.

Two weeks later, I called back to the doctor and advised him that neither worked. To be honest, I could not imagine a circumstance when I would use them.

He said, "There is one foolproof way. I'll give you a syringe and a potent liquid. There are unfortunately two downsides. Firstly, ladies, are not receptive to a man fumbling around trying to find the right vein in which to inject at that sensitive moment.

Secondly, the effects of the injection can last for up to **six hours**. This means "You can't go shopping, visit the dentist, or hairdresser etc soon after the injection!"

An embarrassment I was not willing to suffer.

CHAPTER 15

———— ·•᎗☙᠅☙᠅☙•· ————

Time for a Holiday

A Spell in Paris

Following the prostate operation, I decided to go on a trip to France in 2014.

I was standing in a busy station in Paris (2014) with my bag holding all my important documents and money firmly held between my feet on the floor. As I leaned over to read the train times, I must have taken my eye off my bag.

In just a few seconds I noticed the bag had gone I was filled with horror. All my money and documents… gone! In a busy station! I had thoughts of catching the next flight home. I looked around me. Nothing.

Then I saw a woman with my bag. I was preparing myself for a physical encounter.

She looked at me, smiled, and said, "Is this yours – I'm security and saw this bag on the floor.

I cannot sufficiently explain the extent of my feeling of inner joy and relief at seeing my bag. I went up to the security guard and gave her the biggest hug and kiss I've ever given. She took it all in good spirits. Just as well. I don't usually go around kissing young French women.

After that experience, I stood in one spot completely totally lost. Signs all over the place and hundreds of people going in all directions. I hadn't a clue what to do or where to go.

Just then a smart businessman noticed my distress and came up to me and asked if I needed any assistance. When I explained my situation, he responded, "Follow me."

He then took me up some stairs and then led me to another platform and directed me to a train which we both alighted. Several stations later, he led me off the train and pointed to a bus stop. I then asked where he was going. He responded that he was now going back to his original station.

He had come all this way to assist me in getting to my destination. What a generous and helpful man.

I finally found the hotel (Corail Paris) It was centrally located and allowed me to go to many places without catching the train. The manager really looked after me at breakfast time. He poured out a huge cup of strong coffee for me and kept topping it up. I enjoyed the coffee and emptied each mugful soon after it was filled.

The only problem was that I didn't consider the consequences of so much coffee in one sitting. I chose to walk along the Champs Elysee one morning soon after breakfast, and it wasn't long before I needed to relieve myself. The only problem was that I walked almost the whole of the Champs Elysee but couldn't find a loo anywhere. I was tired and needed to go somewhere badly.

I sat on the grass and resisted the temptation to do something embarrassing just in case a young lady was passing. I finally decided to rush to the station and got home just in time. Lesson learnt – Champs Elysee doesn't have toilets – or they are well-hidden.

In 2019, I went with my son, Daniel to Kuala Lumpur. We were thrilled to find an outstanding vegetarian Indian restaurant just 15-20 minutes away by taxi. This wasn't a bad fare for the driver, so he waited outside the hotel each day to take us there and a further 15-20 minutes to bring us back. The food was so good, that we didn't mind the taxi fares each way.

On the final day, we went for a walk just three minutes away in the opposite direction and found the same restaurant just 150 meters away. We had been paying the taxi to take us on a circular route of many kilometres to a venue just a short walk away.

Our response was the same as with Mr Sharma 33 years ago. We were well and truly done. We laughed openly and unashamedly...and we still do when talking about it.

My Disastrous Love Life

During the long solitary nights, both during Pat's dementia when she was unaware of what was going on around her, and following her death, I sought companionship to fill the void. Like many today, I turned to dating sites or sought companionship on cruises.

Here are true accounts of my experiences, with names changed.

I met Jane on a cruise and since she lived nearby, we met five to six times. Each time she let me foot the bill, without a word of thanks or offering to pay. When I delicately brought up the subject, she retorted that, as a woman, she shouldn't have to pay. We then concluded our relationship. I wonder if she is a relative of Mr Sharma??

Mary whom I met on a dating site, joined me for a meal at the Atrium restaurant, in Perth. We finished eating early, so we went to my house to watch a movie, called "Brassed Off." When the movie ended, she looked at her watch and informed me that she doesn't like driving at night. She then asked me if she could sleep in the spare room at the rear of the house. I agreed and off she went. I was relieved when she went straight to bed.

The next morning, I went for a run, and when I returned, I saw that there was someone in my bed. (To be exact it was the marital bed I shared with my wife when she was alive) I asked, "Is that you, Mary?" She threw off the bedclothes revealing her naked body and made inviting gestures.

I was furious and shouted, "How dare you! Get out of this house now!" Off she went somewhat surprised at my reaction. The next day, she rang me on the phone and requested I call round to her house to help her do some work on her computer. I can't remember exactly what I said but she got the message loud and clear.

I found June on a dating site. First-time dates should start with a coffee. On this occasion, June was keen to miss any preliminaries and have a meal immediately.

"Let's go somewhere nice in South Perth. We'll take it in turns paying. You buy this one and I'll buy the next one," she said. June was charming and attractive. I agreed without hesitation. The only problem was that after the meal, June blocked my number.

My son told me that several men and women get free expensive meals in this manner. And the guilty parties never get caught.

When visiting my wife in her nursing home, I made friends with one of the carers who worked there. I took her out several times, but on each occasion, she was always looking over her shoulder afraid that someone from work would see her.

If caught, she would get the sack. So sad that she worked there for many years but had no outside friends. Where does a lonely carer go to make friends after a stressful day overseeing dementia patients all day long? The only men she ever saw outside that environment were those who visited the nursing home.

CHAPTER 17

Back to China....Again!

For over six years my son, Daniel, had been making his mark in China teaching the English language to Chinese Students. Because of my wife, Pat's slow onset of dementia, and her desire to catch up with Daniel, I decided to visit China by way of a ship. She enjoyed the trip...but the clock was ticking.

We caught up with Daniel and stayed at his apartment. Pat was still alert enough to share in some humour. We needed a boarding pass for our flight home, but Daniel's computer could not print it out. In those days, before everyone had mobile phones, we used internet cafes.

I told Pat, "Come with me. We'll find an internet café." Pat said, "Don't be stupid. This is Beijing, you'll never find one." It was only a short walk before I saw the traditional row of empty computers, available in an internet café. Feeling rather proud to have found an internet café so soon, I confidently led the way in and took a seat.

I was horrified to find that the writing on the screen was in Chinese. So, I called a lady from the back to help. Fortunately, she could speak English. But before she began, she called a lady from the back to bring us each a cup of tea.

We sat down and relaxed with our cups of tea and were in awe of her speed in preparing our documents. When finished, she came over to us and handed us the completed documents.

I put my hand in my pocket to get out some money to give to the lady, and said, "This is the best internet cafe that I've ever been to!"

She replied, **"Sir, this is not an internet café. It's a leasing agency. And you're sitting in my seat!!!"** **Woops!**

Red-faced, we crept out, totally embarrassed. Pat gave me one of her looks, "You wait until we get home".

Dark Years

God's Waiting Room

One of the afflictions we all dread is dementia of one kind or another. I spent five years nursing my wife, Pat, at home, watching her closely to ensure that hot kettles and saucepans etc were kept out of her reach.

Pat knew that she would not be with us for much longer. But she continued to raise a smile. In the early stages of her dementia, she would ring her friend, not realising it was in the middle of the night.

She became increasingly high maintenance, and it came to a breaking point when she would regularly get up in the middle of the night and fall over. She was too heavy to pick up and I had to summon a passer-by in the street to help me get Pat back indoors. I decided it was time to provide her with the close attention that she needed. When I broached the subject of a care facility (Nursing Home), she was very gracious about it and offered no objection.

There were long waiting lists for the Homes, and we were pleased when a friend who owned a nursing home helped us find a place. Pat was the sort of person to make friends with everybody and always greeted them with a smile and a chat.

In the first week, she went around to all the other rooms of clients and introduced herself with her usual smile.

But life in a nursing home is not a normal environment. Many people did not appreciate this strange person greeting them with a smile or Good Morning. They put in a complaint. They wanted to keep to themselves.

So Pat was transferred to another section where many people were too far gone to worry about callers. So, Pat stayed in her room. I visited her twice a day and took her out for a walk in her wheelchair.

Our family watched Pat slowly die over 5-6 years at the nursing home. On one occasion, the local doctor suggested that she be set free from this trauma by withholding her food. It's always easy to make such suggestions for someone else. But not your own wife or mother. We declined. This period of our lives was ten years of hell for the family. The loss knocked us all for six.

Nursing Homes provide care to people with a wide variety of afflictions. There were some very nice people in the Home. It was a pleasure to spend time with them at mealtimes and during the various activities. However, there were a few people who, probably due to some affliction or the result of senility, could be downright rude or nasty. For example, there was one lady, who, when Pat came to the dining room, would say out loud, "Here comes that stupid lady" I tried to give an appropriate response to correct her, but it had no effect. This lady was too far gone to change. Fortunately, it didn't have any effect on Pat. Probably because it didn't register. As I was with Pat most of the time during the day, I was able to steer her clear of such people who could upset her.

The nurses, apart from a few exceptions, were very caring. You would need a considerate nature to work in such an environment.

Pat had reached the stage where she had no control over her bowels. There is only one thing worse than cleaning such a person; it is to have to ask someone to clean you. Pat had passed that stage. I was the one to call for assistance. When she needed cleaning, it was an eye-opener to see how efficiently the carers complete their set routine. Pat was clean and smelt good in just 5 minutes.

The home cares for people of all personalities and backgrounds. There are always those who can't help rankling others. As you entered the corridor, on your right was Dennis (Den for short). He gave the staff a hard time. They hated him and were glad when they had completed any business for him. He would shout

out, "When's my coffee going to come?" or "How much longer is my dinner going to be?"

He would always growl at the staff. Never a smile, nor a please or thank you. One day I was just about to walk past him and decided to stop and talk. I saw he had a beer in his hand and asked, "What beer do you like? I'll go and get you one." He replied, "No need. I've got a fridge full" He then threw one over to me. We must have made a huge impact upon his beer supply because we never stopped talking for several hours. He told me he had been a sailor all his life and never got married.

We both had good knowledge of things and good memories. We discussed music, football, beer, movies etc. We decided to buy a carton of mixed beers from all over the world and score them according to how much we liked them. Each evening, he was waiting for me with beer duly frozen.

One evening just as I arrived, one of the staff called me to one side and asked what I had been doing to put a smile on his face. She said they had never seen him in such a good mood and as a result, there was peace in that section. Very soon my son Daniel also started calling on him on his way through. The nurses said that there was now peace in the section.

One day when I called on Den, he was motionless and had a sheet covering his body and head. A flower was placed in the middle.

One problem with nursing homes is that if you make friends with someone, it won't be long before you must mourn them. So, you always keep that bit of distance.

Meanwhile Pat continued to deteriorate. When she arrived, she could say some sentences. But this gradually went. It wasn't long before she just stared into space and couldn't understand a word or acknowledge our presence.

This was the same Pat that we saw at the beginning of this memoir. I must confess that there is a tear in my eye as I write this as it is now seven years since I lost her, and we were married 54 years.

More on Pat

In all my activities, my wife, Pat. stood by me. Although I spent time away, Pat was always there waiting for me. We were married 54 years and my trips away from Pat were probably less than ten months. She wasn't the typical wife in those days, staying at home and doing all the housework. I believe the following will provide some context and balance to my activities:

Pat went to England many times on her own to visit her parents. As mentioned earlier in this memoir, Pat visited Indonesia on her own to stay with a student, called Rianto. Pat also went to Bali for a holiday with her friend, Mary. On top of all these activities, Pat spent one year with me on the Aboriginal community. She also regularly wined and dined with the lady next door.

And in between all my exploits mentioned in this memoir, Pat and I enjoyed many cruises (Platinum members) and overseas trips together. She generated a comfortable income, which was a buffer for all my exploits. Outside of business, we did everything together. We went out to dinner each week. She was everything to me. I can't remember us ever arguing or raising voices.

It is worth remembering that this is the same Pat that I fought so hard for following the toss of a coin.

CHAPTER 18

Return to Where We Started....

Oh yes. The toss of a coin…Can you see its implications?

What would have happened if that coin had turned up, tails? I would certainly would not have married Pat.

I doubt if I would have emigrated without Pat's support. I certainly wouldn't have all my present children, grandchildren, great-grandchildren.

I would have likely found another wife with a lot of different children. None of the events that occurred in this memoir would have occurred.

And you would not be reading this.

All because of the toss of a coin sixty years ago, which just easily could have come up tails.

In the end, my memoir is not just a recounting of successes and failures, but a testament to the resilience of the human spirit, regardless of how the cards are dealt, or upon which side the tossed coin lands.

Similarity to the Notebook Story.

In the film, Noah was determined to win the girl over. He did crazy things to get a date with her. (Is that familiar?) At the end of the film, we saw his wife with dementia, not remembering him, until she had a moment of remembering. Pat also had the same brief surge of memory when she was nearing the end of her life. On this occasion, it was witnessed by many people.

The similarities with the NoteBook are amazing and some may consider I may have borrowed from the book. The reality is that apart from their earlier years, the similar *events in this memoir occurred long before Nicholas Sparks, the author of The Notebook, was born!*

EPILOGUE

As a young man, I once flipped a coin to decide whether to attend a dance. The coin landed on heads, signalling that I should go. That decision led me to meet my future wife, and despite her initial absence on our first date, my determination led me to search through the Yellow Pages for over an hour to find where she worked. This perseverance paid off, and it's a memory I hold dear.

Throughout my life, I've faced numerous challenges that tested my resolve. When confronted with adversity, I often think back to that Yellow Pages search, reminding myself of the determination that led me to find my wife and make that initial connection. It serves as a poignant reminder that when faced with a challenge, I must remain persistent and resolute.

Similarly, that coin toss wasn't merely chance—it was a toss of destiny, guiding me toward a path I was meant to follow. It serves as a reminder that sometimes, fate has a role in our choices, nudging us toward opportunities we might not have otherwise pursued.

Reflecting on these experiences, I find inspiration in the challenges I've overcome and the determination that guided me. Whether it's navigating the complexities of business or personal relationships, I draw strength from these memories, reminding myself that with grit and perseverance, I can overcome any obstacle.

I'm now well into my eighties and my time on the planet is drawing to a close. I may not be here when you read this memoir.

I hope you have been inspired and gained insights from my active life.

Post Cards

The following are excerpts from Postcards sent home whilst overseas. They are brief primarily due to the personal nature and secondly the writing was too small for my aging eyes.

Excerpt from a card sent from Chicago 16 July 1986

Just passing through Chicago. The building in the picture is said to be the world's tallest. It's still raining here. People in Vancouver were very friendly. Houses were superb and the scenery magnificent. People keep asking if I'm Australian. They say my accent gives me away. Paul Hogan ads are very popular here, (Thankfully I don't speak like him.)

Excerpt from card dated 6 July 1986

I'm I'm on transit from Los Angeles To Corpus Christi, Texas. The men really do wear tall hats and cowboy boots.

Excerpt from a card from Corpus Christi, Texas on 8 July 1986.

Had an interesting day in Mexico yesterday. Many live in a wooden shed no bugger than our hen house. Had a good Mexican meal in one of their top-class restaurants.

Excerpt from a card sent from New York on 14 July 1986

NY is dirty and personal. No one cares if you don't get served. No one smiles, Buildings are grey with grime. Theatres in London are better than those in Broadway.

Excerpt from a card from New York dated 16 July 1986

Had enough of New York. Cars blowing their horns for no reason. Drivers are rude and so are shopkeepers. Never a please or thank you. Change is plonked on the counter Etc.